OLD GIRL

ELSIE JOHNSTONE

Selected poems

by

Elsie Johnstone

Old girl
Copyright © 2024 by Elsie Johnstone
978-0-6453209-2-3

Published by G. & E. Johnstone. All rights reserved. No part of this publication may be reproduced in any manner whatsoever, or stored in a retrieval system or transmitted in any form or by any means, electronic, mechanical, photocopying, recording or otherwise, without the prior written permission of the author, except in the case of brief quotations embodied in critical articles or reviews. Please do not participate in or encourage the piracy of copyrighted materials in violation of authors' rights. Purchase only authorized editions.

The publisher and author assume no responsibility or liability whatsoever on the behalf of any purchaser or reader of this material. Any perceived slight of specific people or organizations is unintentional. While all attempts have been made to verify information provided in this publication, neither the author nor the publisher assumes any responsibility for errors, omissions or contrary interpretation of the subject matter herein.

Old girl - *like the first two books in the trilogy,* Lakes Entrance girl *and* Catholic girl *- is also available as an e-book for Kindle, Kobo, Apple and other devices.*

Dedication

To resilient and wonderful women everywhere, especially those who have accompanied me through my life's journey:

My mother, Kathleen Mary Theresa Allen, and her four joyous sisters (the Bourke girls, Eileen, Maree, Marge and Agnes) who played such a vital and happy role in my childhood.

My six beautiful and resourceful sisters, Margaret (dec), Joan, Kathleen, Maureen (dec), Mary and Eileen, who have been an important part of my life from birth into old age. We shared the same parents, grew up in the same place, ate and yarned around the same dinner table, went to the same schools in the same towns, and yet, we are all so very different. Between us we gave birth to and nurtured twenty-seven little Aussies, all different, all wonderful.

My three fun-loving and able daughters, Caitlin, Tessa and Eloise, who amaze me every day with their wisdom, joy for life, resilience and the ability to give and receive love.

My core friends, Libby, Wendy, Leona and Trina. We met in the Maternity Section of the Sandringham Hospital over forty-five years ago. We have shared the journey, have been constant and non-judgmental playmates and confidantes though the thick and thin of motherhood and beyond. Every woman needs a group of mates like you guys.

The women of my generation who fought for the rights of all women to be free agents. Thank you, you stood up and made your voices heard.

The two important men in my life, Graeme and Chris, husband and son. Good men provide the yin to women's yang, the mutual respect and support that makes the world a fairer place.

And the young women of today. Don't give up the hard-earned rights; gender equality is still but a dream.

Keep fighting.

- Elsie Johnstone.

Contents

INTRODUCTION 1

ON AGEING

Old girl 2
What do other people see? 3
Me knees have gone! 4
Back then 5

ON FAMILY

Can we bottle babies? 6
My favourite place 7
Off to the beach 8
A special friendship 9
You don't own your children 10

ON POLITICS

The day the Prime Minister said "Sorry" 12
The Queen is dead 14
Political correctness 15
The minefield of gender fluidity 16

ON WOMEN

Old woman 17
Girls beware! 18
What about us Aussie women? 19
Women, stand up and be counted 22
Mother 23
Mothers-in-law 24
Elder abuse 25

ON PHILOSOPHY

I now know the answers 26
Pebble in the pond 27
Death comes to us all 28
Opinion 29
Karma 30
It's how the cards fall 31
My mother's advice 32
Let it ride 33

ON LIFE

The Top Ten fallacies during my lifetime 34
How sad is this? 37
The office sleazebag 38
Open For Inspection 39
When did the world become so complicated? 40
Telecommunication, a journey 42
Pending storm 44

ON LOVE

Ideal man 45
The ark of love 46
Old love 47
Two ducks 48
The Yarram Football Club Ball 49

ON MELBOURNE

Melbourne in spring time 50
Melbourne in winter 51
Melbourne in autumn 52
Melbourne on a summer's day 53
Melbourne, the world's most liveable city 54
Beautiful Beaumaris by the sea 55

ON REFLECTION

Why? 56
Bounce-back-ability 56
Lucky us 57
I am Aussie 58
Simple things 60

AND FINALLY

The anchor poems 61

OTHER WORKS 62

Introduction

Australia's young people are better educated than any previous generation.

They simply lack life experience.

And that's what we oldies have in spades!

A store of wisdom acquired over a lifetime of living, making mistakes and experiencing 'aha' moments.

Let me tell you about it!

- EJ.

ON AGEING

Old girl

In this day and age where we worship youth
It is ridiculed to be long in the tooth
Nobody wants to be old, age is most unattractive
And it matters not whether agile and active
The young folk look at us oldies with wonder
Was getting old a dreadful blunder, were these old folk ever younger?

How on earth did they come to this frightening stage?
God, I hope I don't look like that when I age!
They groan when they bend down to fix their shoes
And what's all of this about an afternoon snooze?
Why walk so slow, the pace of a sick snail
And you need our help with phones and email

And that's not the end of it
What's with those comfy shoes with the extra-wide fit?
Why so much effort to dress, get out of chairs
Hear the television, climb the stairs?

My answer is that I am not simply aging
I'm maturing, ripening and changing
Sweet fruit ready for the harvest
Have had the best of life, but eager for the rest
Being young is not a protection from growing old
Over that nobody has control
The only alternative to aging is death
It's not 'curtain closed' until you breathe your last breath

What do other people see?

What do other people see
When they stand back and look at me?
They mostly see an old lady, rickety and bent
An old, ancient woman whose life is nearly spent

What do my neighbours observe
When I negotiate the curb?
Do they detect signs of deterioration?
Estimate my time draws near for cremation?

What about the shopkeepers I meet
When I go walking down the street
Do they ignore and fail to greet me
Discreetly overlook me completely
To serve others in the store
Who will spend a good deal more?

My grandchildren love me but have no doubt
That my life is done, I'm soon due to check out
They see a darling old soul
They are young while I am old

My children see their dear old Mum
Who is not quite as useful and not quite as much fun
They see aging bones but wish to deny it
As long as they can, they tend to blind eye it

My husband sees a beautiful young bride
His one true love, his joy and pride
He remembers cosy dinners by the fire
Waking up side by side, hearts filled with desire
He remembers mucking in, making a home together
Of happy days, sad days, days fraught with stormy weather
Bushwalks, Christmas shopping, swimming in the surf
Little kids, nurturing and caring, giving for all its worth
He sees partners and new babies welcomed to the clan
A comfortable companion, the one who understands
The relentless march almost completed together
Our journey of life through good and bad weather
Now at life's terminus he lovingly holds my hand
His bride became an old woman, her groom an old man

Me knees have gone!

I don't know when it happens, but it seems to creep up on you
Suddenly, you're not moving the way you used to do
Instead of bouncing off the chair
And taking off without a care
You now are slow and measured, can't be pressured
Push back, push up, stand, straighten, pause and you're away
The trouble is, it's taken half the day

It's me knees, you see, they don't want to hold me
And if they do, they rattle and scold me
And ache for hours while I try to get some sleep
'Til I get out of bed and round the house creep
Searching for a Panadol
To get the pain under control

I don't understand it, I don't know what I've done
I know I am squat, and somewhat rotund
But I never abused my knees, I never tried to run
I wasn't one to mountain climb or ski
Or play sports that put pressure on the knee

Although …
I went through a religious phase, in retrospect
When I knelt to pray or to genuflect
I was young then and my joints behaved
But by praying so that my soul would be saved
And by speaking too much to Jesus
I've gone and ruined me old knees'us

Back then

Back then, we weren't always politically correct
That I regret, it caused great pain
We didn't throw our laundry in the dryer
We hung it on the line, even in the rain

Back then, children were expected to be quiet and pleasant, especially around adults
Can't say whether that was to show respect, or was it to hide their faults?

Back then, fizzy drinks or fruit juice was reserved for special occasions
Water was our drink of choice from the bubble-tap in the playground

Back then, we simply mucked around with balls, marbles, yo-yos and sticks
Played outside with a skipping rope, and practised all sorts of tricks

Back then, if there was somewhere we needed to go we would ride a bike or walk
The telephone was on the wall and we had to pay to talk

Back then we went to church on Sunday to be lectured by the preacher
He told us the rules and what to think and thought he was our teacher

Back then, the government would do what they do and no one took much note
Except for a few weeks every three years when we all turned out to vote

Back then we'd have fish and chips on a Friday night, other meals were cooked at home
We would only dine out on special occasions and never ate on our own

Back then we mostly drank tea, made in a billy, a kettle or a teapot
Coffee was a foreign drink enjoyed only by that New Australian lot

Back then holidays were at an aunt's place or in a town close to us by the sea
Occasionally we would take a road trip to see what we could see

The world is a different place now than it was in the olden days
But dig down deep and the people you meet continue to amuse and amaze
Philosophies may deviate from yours, whether it's left or right wing
People are generally good and kind
We all try to do the right thing.

ON FAMILY

Can we bottle babies?

What joy! Watching babies you know, develop, find their wings and grow
From little Joseph to full blown Joe, and little Florence to grown up Flo
Oh, that we could bottle the essence of young ones up to ten
Sweet and innocent, full of love and joyful positive Zen

A newborn, quaint and soft, choc-a-block with promise
That sweet smell of mother's breast milk and little baby vomit
Those first wee smiles beguile, as Baby recognises and salutes you
Ensures you are slave for life and whatever it takes, you will do

Those wonderful 'aha' moments as Baby discovers new things
Adding daily to the learning blocks, the roundabouts and swings
Learning to roll, creep and crawl, off from the mat and into the hall
Baby takes off, his world to explore, patter of hands and feet on the floor

The most precious times in a toddler's life are so fleeting and sweet
A walk to the shops, small hand in yours, chatting all the way down the street

Off to school where other kids rule, the peer group becomes so important
Lessons to learn, accolades to earn, little mind alert and absorbent
So many new things to discover, learns there is more than just his mother
The world is a big place, but home is still base, an all-important background
Watch them grow as their seeds they sow, secure you will always be around
Until they mature, not children any more, school is done and with luck they blossom
You see your reward, what you have been aiming toward
Baby is now Captain Awesome

My favourite place

Warm and cosy, snug and toasty
Fresh clean sheets, pillows soft and floaty
When everything is done and it has all been said
I simply love my bed

At the end of even the worst of days
After work, and play, whatever the malaise
My own sweet heaven, close my eyes and wait to see
What dreams the dream maker has in store for me

In that time before awake becomes asleep
When the body unwinds, and all cares released
Trust my worries to my brain knowing answers will be found
Upon waking up next day there will be solutions all around
Then into the deep, dark cave of oblivion
I creep to my daily Elysium

When birds herald the new day
I snuggle down further and I stay
Refusing to be prised from my bed
I love it here, I need more sleep, but instead
The alarm rings, the radio blares
Time to get up and go downstairs
Begin preparations for the day ahead
When I'd much rather stay in bed
And forget about the day and all
But then, I'd miss that moment, when into bed at night I fall

Off to the beach

The weekend is here, time to relax
Light up the barbie, don your hats
Grab your tranny, fill the Esky with food
Crack a tinny, bring the dog
Thongs, sunnies, wet suits, prawns in an ice bucket
Sunshine, sand and surf are free, no need for a budget
Pack boogie boards, head for the shores to spend the day
Wet a line, the sea is our shrine, surf the waves, let's play
Come on let's go! Beware the strong under tow!
Relax under the umbrella and daydream
Examine the facts and it would seem
That a day at the beach is the Aussie dream

You don't own your children

The older I get the more I recognise the reality
That the most precious gift of all is our own fertility
Which allows us to reproduce our family genes
To make little babies, tiny kings and queens

Each precious bundle gives us purpose, something to strive for
A bucket load of love and fun, something to remain alive for

Each baby born to the family brings
A garland of flowers and sparkling rings
An entire orchestra full of wonderful things
A little person so unique
And full of mystique
A precious gift to carefully un-tweak

The common fault many parents make
Is to regard a child as their personal keepsake
A little mini me to shape
To which they own exclusive rights
For love, loyalty and control for life

Our babies are only ours on loan
To love and care for in our home
Develop talents, personality and intellect
Give our love and care, treat with respect
To nurture and nourish until adulthood
Baby belongs to himself, that should be understood

And if adult children enjoy time with us, it's a choice, not a chore
It's because love and admiration has been earned, nothing more

A special friendship

Baby boomers enjoying seduction
Giving birth to our bubs, full reproduction
Babies galore, pretty young mums
Pink and blue cupids, sweet dimpled bums

A new experience, so very exciting
Also, quite scary and ever so frightening
Welcome to a different world
Learn to swaddle tightly
Is the nappy soiled?
It was all a mystery to us
But we dare not make a fuss
For we were supposed to intuitively know
What to do and where to go
How to navigate this bus

We were blessed to be five Sandy Hospital girls
Supporting each other with the twists, turns and swirls
Loving our babies, as they laugh, sing and play
But once home on our own, there was no nurse to whisk them away

We girlfriends compared notes, shared the little we knew
Navigated sleep times and the sweet-smelling breast milk spew
Sure, we made mistakes, that we cannot deny
We confessed, and made fun of them
If we didn't laugh, we'd cry

We shared our dreams and fears and tales, each one with the other
There is no rule book that has been writ for when a woman becomes mother
We did our best with all we knew
Our intentions good but often screwed
That's when our group came into their best
The child's survival, the only litmus test

Through many years we navigated this maze
Indulged the children with every craze
Birthdays, milestones, outings to the park
We made it fun, it was such a lark
If help was called for, we were there to assist
No need for counselling, we were our own psychiatrists
Through good times and the disappointing and sad
My friends stopped each other going stark, raving mad

Somewhere along the line we turned the bus
The focus changed. It became more about us
Wine time, celebrations, weekends, lunches and anniversaries
Girlfriends, playmates, counsellors, whatever the needs be

It takes a long time to grow an old friend
How could we have known how well it would end?
Our babies grew up, and at the end of the day
We consider, that in the circumstances, we did OK
Probably, if asked, that's not what the kids would say!

Now they're doing their best with all that they know
Just like we did. They give it a go.
It seems only yesterday, but half a century has passed
And that's an awful long time for any friendship to last

ON POLITICS

The day the Prime Minister said "Sorry"

On the thirteenth day of February, 2008
Darwin town was abuzz with anticipation
Because the Prime Minister of this great nation
Had made a date, down in Canberra, to say
Sorry, mate, we didn't mean to offend you
We Europeans thought we were the superior race
We were simply trying to mend you
We thought what we were doing was colonisation
Perhaps we were wrong, if that's any consolation
So I'm saying, "Sorry."

We thought you'd appreciate our Christian values
That your Aboriginality you would gladly lose
To live and think like white man does, by our moral code
Never thought of the ancient culture we would unwittingly decode
We isolated you on Christian missions
Stole your slave labour without any permissions
We settlers saw it as colonisation
Now we have come to the realisation
That it wasn't right, so we say, "Sorry."

We dressed you in uniforms, oversaw your work and prayer
Stole your children and quietly left them where
They were hidden from you, and as they grew
Never had the chance to be taught all you knew
We assimilated and deflated you, damaged and berated you
We saw it as colonisation
But now have reached the realisation
That it was wrong, so we are sorry

We shattered your identity and all beliefs spiritual
Our European ways on you imposed
Because we supposed
They were superior to traditional Aboriginal ritual
We introduced hard-hoofed animals and exotic plants and trees
Subjected you to massacre and devastating disease
Caused widespread hunger, malnutrition and death
Left your tribal culture and way of life bereft
It's a bit late, but, "Sorry mate!"

We built fences to demonstrate that the land was ours
Filled those paddocks with our own sheep and cows
Destroying native fauna and flora
And everything else that went before you
Thought it was colonisation
But have reached the realisation
That it was wrong, so we are sorry

On that long awaited day in February
Mobs left country to flood into town
The Top End Parliament was full, no room to sit down
Crowded into the Main Hall
Wanting to be a part of it all
Telling stories of broken families and culture torn apart
Women raped, tribes slaughtered
It happened from the very start
Now from Canberra they admit it was not colonisation
It was an invasion
A cultural annihilation

For over sixty thousand years my people cared for this nation
Nurturing the land, honouring its creation
White man decimated our communities, culture, language and hunting grounds
Checked us out for dirt, grime and headlice, and tough as it sounds
Stripped us of our freedom, autonomy and every civil right
Promoted assimilation, tried to make us white
Absorbed us, scorned us, forced us to the brink of extermination
Denied us many privileges enjoyed by the rest of the nation
Leading us to our current sad plight
Where we suffer from hunger
Die much younger
It's just not right

Platitudes are easy to give
They amount to nought if we can't live
With self-respect and autonomy
In our own country
So that once again we can be
Proud and strong Aborigine

To say "Sorry" is great
And we accept it as graciously given, mate
But it all amounts to nothing
If all we get is white man's huffing and puffing

The Queen is dead

The Queen is dead
Long live the King
What have we Aussies been fed?
What is this thing?
The institution of the English monarchy
What has it to do with me?
Show me the so-called blue blood of the King
Is the colour different from mine?
Its composition more refined?

Has the Almighty in his infinite love
Sent him to us, deigned he is superior
Exalted him above all others
Personally appointed him our Emperor
A gift from the heavens above?

Or is it a hoax?
A clever series of master strokes?
To dress a man in jewels and flowing cloaks
Pretty him up with medals and the like
All sorts of regalia shining bright
In parades with horses who have their manes in plaits
Ridden by men in red with black furry hats

Spin a good yarn, relate a fairy-tale
Of how without this man, the realm will fail
And how the monarch is good for us
Into his hands we should put our trust
He cannot falter, he has God on his side
Let's forget colonisation and all the genocide
That happened when other lands were declared
The realm of the king, not to be shared
Is it sane to swear our trust
To a man
No better or worse than I am
And grant him permission to reign over us?

Political correctness

Politically correct speech shapes
The way our world communicates
Political correctness tells us what to think and believe
What we can do, how we achieve
Not good enough these days to be tardy
Simply rescheduled your arrival time
The insane are not crazy, mad or foolhardy
Reality challenged is the new paradigm
A lazy sod is motivationally deficient
These tags are verbose and so inefficient
When did the worst become least best?
Lies are now alternative facts, that too fails the test
A metabolically over-achiever used to be simply fat
An abundantly verbal person was talkative, now how about that?
We're told to use gender neutral terms, them and they instead of he or she
Thus, we avoid assumptions regarding one's identity
In endeavours to limit confrontation, avoid aggravation and become more free
The ultimate irony it seems to me
Is the loss of freedoms, fought for and won
Are sidelined and vilified, one by one
Debate silenced, creates discord and suspicion
We lose language, culture, freedom of expression

The minefield of gender fluidity

Once it was simple when the world began
At birth one was assigned to be either woman or man
Adam was Adam, and Eve was Eve
She gave him an apple which caused much grief
Today, that simplicity is so over-rated
It's no longer elementary, it's more complicated

They say there are thirty-three genders with which to identify
Reject what you are now, select one and diversify
Cisgender is highly under-rated
It is simply male or female, as assigned; it's uncomplicated
Then there is demigender, intergender, agender
With or without gender
Genderfluid or genderqueer
Pangender, polygender, omnigender
Or somewhere in the middle, as long as you're sincere

Androgyne identifies with neither masculine and feminine
Choose somewhere on spectrum, then simply draw the line
You can be gender non-conforming
By physically and emotionally reforming
Tri-gender shifts between the male, female and some other difference
While an intersex with mixed anatomy may express a preference
To identify with the opposite sex
But then it becomes much more complex
It's all so complicated and it really matters not
Accept yourself for what you are, without getting others in a knot

ON WOMEN

Old woman

For me, life isn't a frantic steeplechase to win first place
I simply want to grow old with grace
Progress through life with no undue stress
Without too much pain, worry or distress
While savouring the joys and highlights
Surviving the knockbacks, sorrows and lowlights
At the end I will die happy and content
Consider my time on earth was well spent
If I leave behind strong people who love, share and care
And in whose lives' journey I had the privilege to share
I laughed, so my face is aged and wrinkled
I cared, so my head with grey hairs is sprinkled
I enjoyed food and wine, so my teeth are wonky
My hearing is faded, and my knees are shonky
I now view life from my old age grandstand
And believe me, life never goes exactly as planned
You can die young and have a good-looking corpse
Or do the journey, get old and have no remorse
I'd ask that you consider the alternative
So don't complicate things, keep it simple, just live
Smile and laugh take the good with the bad
Don't waste time being too angry or sad
Learn from our animals who live life as it comes
Hunt for their needs, care for their little ones
You can squander your life by overthinking it
So be true to yourself, avoid hoodwinking it!

Girls beware!

Girls, we have come a long way, but I'm telling you now
There is still much to be done before we slay the sacred cow
Of male supremacy and men's sense of propriety
And the way they cling to the patriarchal society

When I was young
The song that was sung
Was that we women were lesser beings
An inferior sex
Emotions unchecked
Intellectually weak and unhinged

The man ruled the roost
We girls there to boost
His ego and see to his needs
Never to shirk doing the work
Be an incubator for his seed

A girl's life at birth
Was the sum of her worth
And was laid out for her on a platter
No right to a career
Or an academic year
Why on earth would all of that matter?

Ideas beyond station
Would end in frustration
And only cause much strife
Education is a jewel
Wasted on a girl
She'll just be mother and wife

Look around us today
And some will say
We really don't need to fight any more
But you women beware
Don't let down your hair
Gaining equality is still no pushover

It's simply not so
And I'm letting you know
That the battle is definitely not over
Men have had everything
And are on a good thing
And would like to keep it that way

They love their status
Supplied to them gratis
And when you look closely
Why wouldn't they?

So girls, don't give up the fight
Demand equal rights
Dig right in, say your piece, and do your thing
What is mostly true
Is the world belongs to you
Equally as much as it does to him

What about us Aussie women?

It seems mighty strange that all Aussies are expected to know
That Don Bradman is famous, because he played a game a century ago
About the same time, Edith Cowen and Enid Lyons are largely unsung entities
Because the men made the rules and viewed them as fools, only good for pouring teas
These women fought for equity and justice, shaping Australia's formation
And while doing great things they managed to birth seventeen children for our great nation

The female cohort is largely ignored, succumbing to male domination
But we do exist, so let's insist, that we are included in the Aussie equation
Give us a voice, ask what is our choice, and consider what makes us tick
Do guys ever wonder, what it's like down under, to be a chick without a dick?

Aussie girls are ambitious, they study hard to forge a good career
They tend to look outwards to the world, love travel, far and near
Mums and girls play their sport, simply for the love of the game
Without sponsorships enjoyed by the boys, we turn up just the same
In our thousands to play netball every Saturday of the year

Aussie girls frequent live music because they love to dance
Hoping that along the way, by chance, they will find true romance
We gather in groups to enjoy a laugh, a chat and good company
Girls' night out, girls' night in, girls' weekend in the country

We ladies enjoy a glass of chardy, perhaps champers at our book club
Have you got the gossip, where did you hear that, what exactly is the rub?
Ladies like tracky dacks and Uggs at home on a winter's day
Curled up by the fire with a book while the men watch the footballers play
What happens when the ladies get together? I am unable to tell
Birds of a feather, secret women's business, if revealed it would send me to hell
We women are good for driving the boat, keeping it afloat, while the men ski along behind
We help put up the tent, know what money's been spent, and do what is asked as assigned

We take a pav to the barbie, it's our job to source the steak and the snags
We make the salads, prepare the feast and leave the cooking up to the lads
Kids love Savoy bikkies with Vegemite, the men like Sao and cheese
Ladies tend to know all of this stuff and try their best to fulfil everyone's needs
It certainly seems that we are on top of most things and add lots to Aussie culture
We live our own life and are much more than wife, daughter, sister and mother
We girls add the spice, and let's be precise, we keep the show on the road
If we were to sit, and not do our bit, Australia would surely implode

Women, stand up and be counted

We women are constantly overlooked and discounted
It's time! Stand up and be counted
Speak with authority
We are not a minority
As fifty-one percent of the population
We demand equal participation
In all that goes on in our great nation

Alcohol-fuelled testosterone
And blatantly sexist undertone
False loyalty to the boys' club
Take care of a mate, drink in the pub
While deadbeat dads disappear
Cover the little child's ears, so he doesn't hear

Let's demand proper standards of human behaviour
Progress, kindness, empathy and sharing of power
Women are not conquests
To be treated as objects
Girls, take your place, treat the world as the men do
It's your own domain, to do what you want to

If right is on your side, don't flinch at all
Abide by your principals, stand straight and tall
Look the world straight in the eyes
Refuse to back down or apologise
We are more than half of the world's population
Demand equal rights to participation
In all that goes on in every nation

Mother

Can you ever be prepared for losing a mother
Who knew you and loved you like no other?
Her heart beat accompanied your first journey
From embryotic being to small baby on the knee
You recognised her voice before all others
She gifted you with your sisters and brothers
Your mother whose eyes knew your every feature
Your mother, your life source, your very first teacher

No matter how old at death she might be
She was the one who thought of you constantly
Who was there for you every day of her life
And supported you through trouble and strife
She scolded you when she thought you untoward
Holding your hand while you played life's chess board
She was the mum whose counsel you often rejected
But that she accepted; her love unaffected
She loved you unconditionally
She wanted you to be your 'very best me'
Oh, what a huge gap she leaves now she is gone
But in you and your children she continues to live on

Mothers-in-law

Mothers-in-law get bad publicity
Daughter in law proclaims, 'She drives me crazy!'
No matter what she does or how hard she tries
She can never do the right thing in the young wife's eyes
Why is the first person to be shown the door
Is your son's wife's mother-in-law?
What makes her the target of derision?
That no respect is applied to her position?
She birthed the son that she nurtured and cared for
Taught him to respect, how to love, all the things he stands for
Gifted him as a grown man on his wedding day
She doesn't want him back, or to take him away
From the family he's made that is so dear to her heart
It's her worst nightmare that those two should part
She is his mother, having nurtured him since infancy
But her job is done, he's her mate now, he loves her differently
She is not the opposition
She knows her position
She is on the side of the young bride
There to love and support, not to move her aside
She'll never be *her* mother, that special bond they share
But respect that he loves *his* mum, treat her with love and care
Please make it easy for mother-in-law to be part of the fun
In the beautiful family that you two have begun
Love and respect me as your beloved's mum

Elder abuse

She lived in the same neighbourhood as me
Our lives crossed and I could not help but see
She worked for her family diligently
Contributed to the community

A woman of faith, she honoured her husband and deferred to him
To do anything less she would have considered a sin
But in her family of men, the feminine view was not recognised
Her opinion was minimised, she was totally disenfranchised

The husband died suddenly, a huge shock to the family
In her grief she was bullied, her sons sensed her fragility
They could not wait to inherit her money
They teased her and poked her, they thought it was funny

She became disoriented, cranky, felt all alone
Her sons placed her in care, moved her out of her home
They leased it out to pay the expensive fees
When she wanted to cook and tend her own needs

She absolutely hated her unfortunate situation
She begged and implored, gave into frustration
They took all her power and made her feel poor
When, in fact she was not that at all.

Before too long the sons got their way
She relinquished the fight to have her say
She declined, suffered a stroke and took to her bed
Her money was theirs, their mother was dead

ON PHILOSOPHY
I now know the answers

Age can make you wise as you revise your life and the things you've done
I call it wisdom but, in our system, it's presumed that if you are old, you are dumb
By now I know most of the answers, just about the whole damn score
Trouble is nobody bothers to ask me the questions any more

If asked to dispense a small piece of common sense, this is what I would tell them
Have a go, with all that you know, and if you make mistakes wear them
Life is a conga line of decisions, one leading to another
If you stuff the first one up, you can land in lots of bother

You choose your own adventure and have to make your own way
Yesterday's outcomes always affect what happens to you today
For every choice you make, there's the risk of a mistake
So, if at first you fail, learn, reflect and do a retake

You can learn from other people's mistakes, but we rarely do
Everybody does stupid things, no mistake is new
When you do blunder be careful not to fall
Learn from it, move right on
Put it behind you to reflect upon
But remember, the biggest mistake that you can make
Is to never make a mistake at all

Pebble in the pond

When we drop a pebble into a pond
Something happens to reflect upon
Splash! Splatter! Spatter!
Circles within circles are created
Until it can't be estimated
How many tiny surges move on and out
North and south, all about
Rings extending, the motion unending
Waves dancing encore upon encore
Ending, with a silent splash to the shore

Death comes to us all

I've been around for a long time, more than the biblical three score and ten
I reckon I have seen it all, just can't remember where and when
Nothing in the world is new, everything has happened before
Sometimes that is so long ago that we don't remember it any more

There have always been those that do and others that don't
Some who are willing to go the extra mile and some who simply won't
The revolving door spins round and round for each upcoming generation
When old things seem new again, each a wondrous revelation
Making the young ones feel unique
Believing that the world is theirs to tweak

The thing that is constant over the generations
Is that people are mostly good and kind, although there are always abominations
Those who think they are mini-gods, that they are superior
They walk all over their fellow man whom they see as inferior
In the mighty quest for money and power
Anything in their paths is theirs to devour

They imagine Mother Nature will never call their bluff
That they are made from different stuff, so strong and tough
And will live forever, never die, never be eulogised
I ask, how can they be so unwise so as not to realise
Death visits us all and stamps its absolute finality
On our frail mortality

No matter how important you believe you are
What house you live in, how flash is your car
We are all equal when we breathe our last breath
Power, wealth and possessions mean nothing at death
Money can't buy peace of mind, happiness or health
Death comes to us all, no matter what your wealth

Opinion

Opinion is just opinion; neither right or wrong
A comment upon the world and what is going on
With a personal view thrown into the mix
About politics, family and society, an ever-changing bag of tricks
Personal opinion depends upon how one views the game
No two people's opinions are ever exactly the same
They depend on the rules, where are the boundaries?
The environment it's phrased in, personal memories
Opinions can be discussed, altered and debated
When another person states a view, conversation is created
But don't allow the cacophony of other people's noise
Limit your choices, drown your inner voice
Some people argue on subjects when they know little about it
They boldly espouse their view, tout it, flout it
Shout it, get into a fight
But just because they disagree with you
Doesn't mean that you're not right!

Karma

One thing I have discovered
The truth I've uncovered
Please don't let it alarm you
Life is a mix
Of a huge bag of tricks
Some things are good and others will harm you
There can be no doubt
That good and bad you give out
Will come back to you as pure Karma
Karma is law of cause-and-effect
Our behaviours inter-connect
And actions influence our future
If by chance
Your life is askance
It's past actions that are returning to haunt you
How we act does count
It's our life's bank account
it's never too late to atone
As all is not set in stone
Consequences for our actions intersect
Always treat other people with respect

It's how the cards fall

Life is like a game of cards
The luck of the draw is where it all starts
At conception you are already a winner
You won life because your sperm was a fast swimmer

Life is wonderful, it is a gift to be alive
But then come complications, the need to survive
The fall of the cards is the life we are born into
Our parents, our family, our home, our country
Working class, middle class, pauper or gentry
Your genes, your history, the way they accept you
Have you been blessed with good health?
Is your family agog with wealth?
Did they love and nurture you?
Open up paths for you?

Life is not always determined by the fall of the cards
Play your best suit, try to limit discards
The opening hand has been dealt to you
But, by playing your cards right there's things you can do
To alter the progress of the game, all hands are not played the same
Count your cards, keep track of what's gone
Let some tricks go, but for some, take a chance on

When the game is over it's time to tote up
Was it a total muck-up, a complete and utter stuff-up?
Or were you lucky enough to make the right calls
Leading with wisdom and surviving short falls?
Did you have back-up trumps or renege on your partner?
Did you play fair and honest, could your game have been smarter?

My mother's advice

The secret to a happy life, my mother once told me
Is to settle my bills and what I owe and to remain completely debt free
Don't go working up a tab
Only spend the coin that you have
Be beholden to nobody so that you remain free
Work hard, be thrifty, take your cues from the honey bee
Who works from dawn to dusk for the good of the hive
That's why he's on earth, that's why he's alive

For every dollar that you earn, spend only ninety cents
Save the rest for a rainy day, that is common sense
Refrain from buying what you can't afford
Instead, save up and savour the reward
So when you walk from the shop the item is yours
Live by your wits and your own resources
Value independence, care for yourself and your own
Always remember, charity begins at home

Be aware of who you are and stand straight and tall
Be proud of where you come from, don't try to have it all
Don't be jealous of anyone else
Envy gets you nowhere, rely on yourself
Sleep well at night and don't worry
The past is gone and the future will come in a hurry
Today is all you have, so take one day at a time
Do your best, that's all you can do, and things will turn out fine

Let it ride

Let it ride, shrug it off
Dismiss it as fake news
If it is wrong and we don't call it out
It is still injustice and abuse

It's not our business, darling
Purely a domestic matter
That man in his home is the king
She is *his* wife to batter

Ignore the starving animal
He does not belong to you
It's his master's job to treat him right
There's nothing we can do

Oh, isn't it shocking
That fighting in Ukraine
While big powers stoke the fire
We shut our eyes again

Avert thine gaze away from there
To the ethnic cleansing in Palestine
In a David and Goliath clash
Children die and suffer once again

Innocent folk are starving
But that's happening over there
Our own kids are doing well
No need for us to care

Cast a blind eye at institutional abuse
It was another time and era
Those men can't be judged for what went on
Nothing to account for here

Dear Mother Nature is hurting
We must conserve natural resources
In order to stop climate change
But that's a race for other horses

Our world is a hard stage to play
It takes a brave heart to intercede
Refuse bullies their own selfish way
Speak up when there is a need

ON LIFE

The Top Ten Fallacies during my lifetime

1770
Australia was an empty when Cook planted his flag in the sand
What he neglected to say
That before that day
Indigenous peoples had thrived on this land

1910s
In 1914, at the behest of King George
Our soldiers fought the war to end wars
But now we all know
That that wasn't so
Politicians use conflict to enhance
Their image, take a strong stance
However dubious the cause

1960s
A civil war in Vietnam was our concern, due to the Domino Theory
If one country should fall
In time we would all
Be sprouting Communist ideology

The president and the black man were shot by bullets from random snipers
But the CIA know
That this is not so
They dared to be freedom fighters

1970s
As we watched the 70s unfold
We citizens were told
Wars are good and our side has moral authority
To ravage and kill in foreign lands to promote liberal democracy

Until this day, I have nothing to say but that
Offshore war does nothing but harm
Leaders quote 'national security'
When in reality
Their aim is to sell weapons and arms

1980s
We were warned, the world would become
Over-populated and none would survive
But if all things are fair
And each had his share
There is sufficient to keep all alive

All through the ages, our political sages warn
Various countries despise and would harm us
The ultimate aim
Of this evil game
Is to frighten and to alarm us

1990s
By the year 1990, sociologists told us
Technology would deliver more leisure
Who could have foreseen
That these machines
Would put us under more pressure?

Before the millennium, widespread concern warned the Bug would create much ado
Big money was spent
The year came and went
Nothing happened, it was all ballyhoo

2000s
The Pope is infallible, a mouthpiece of God and what he says is the absolute truth
Ha! We may have believed
Had we not been deceived
By bad priests abusing our youth

Refugees fleeing from famine and war get an icy reception
Let's face the fact
That not far back down the track
We are all migrants, with First Nations people, the exception

Reorganise the world, the climate is changing
Our way of living needs rearranging
That was the cry of experts scientific
Who saw melting ice caps and rising tides in the Pacific
Our government declared this a fallacy, concocted to scare
We have coal and gas to sell, so why should we care?

The virus came and went and had us worried
Whole cities locked down
People forbidden to move around
A lazy lab in China and flying bats were to blame
Thus re-enforcing the "We can't trust China" game

The King has blue blood and was born to rule
And this passes through generations
But if the truth be known
His right to the thrown
Is no more than God's other creations

After nearly four score years and with my life almost done
I am here to warn you that there will always be some
Who will do anything to win money, control and power
Do your own research and question if there is ever any doubt
Think for yourself, and it it's wrong, don't be afraid to call it out

How sad is this!

What's with the language?
Does it have to be crude
Once 'not to give a fuck'
Was considered uncouth and rude
And it still is, as far as I can see
Especially when 'not giving a fuck'
Is directed at me

There was once a time
When people were kind
And actually cared about each other
Friends and neighbours were respected
Good manners practised and expected
Only a schmuck wouldn't deign to bother

Now the modern philosophy
Is don't waste your sympathy
On anything other than you
Dismiss others completely
On the surface quite sweetly
Just do what you want to do

This 'I don't give a fuck' world
The 'you don't measure up' world
Is centred purely round 'me'
But 'not giving a fuck' can work two ways, you know
And quickly change a once good friend to a foe
A person can become sorely pissed
If placed upon your 'don't give a fuck' list
And somewhere not far down the track
I will 'not give a fuck' right on back

The office sleazebag

By Jeez
He's a sleaze
Cross your knees
He's old enough to be my father
I'd much rather
Eat cold shit
Than to have any part of him or it!
Keep away from him, they warn
He loves to rub you 'gainst his horn
If he finds you alone in the stationery storeroom
He'll try to show off his family heirloom
He gets his rocks off by harassing you
Has no morals; values askew
Thinks we women are there at his beckoning
So, don't work late without first checking
That he has gone home
And you're alone
He's the office sleaze
So just be careful please!

Open For Inspection

Open For Inspection is today at 2.45
Can't have the family home looking like a dive
Only two weeks into the campaign and I'm almost out of puff
I have polished sinks, cleaned the bath, but have I done enough?
I have decluttered the shelves and benches and have them shining bright
And hidden all evidence of our life here, put it out of sight
I have ensured the wet areas are all spick-and-span
Stored away the chopping boards and dusted the ceiling fan
I have vacuumed up the cat's fur and mopped the kitchen floor
Prettied up all the bedrooms, but wait, there's even more
My hands are sore, my knees do ache from rub and scrub and wash
But at least my trusty family home now looks elegant and posh
I have gathered up the gardening tools and stored them in the shed
Trimmed back the shrubs and plants, so they don't dangle on your head
The cobwebs are gone, the dusting's done, but there's still a smell that lingers on
I know, introduce *more* aromas so as to confuse
Put bread in the oven, light sweet smelling candles
Allow them all to diffuse

When did the world become so complicated?

When did the world become so complicated?
When did simple become complex?
What happened to sitting down and writing a letter
Instead of firing off a quick text?

I have cash in my pocket and wish to make a purchase
Happy to pay the price, but would like a bit of service
I request help but none comes forth, they really make it hard
And finally, when I make a choice, the machine won't take cash, just card

And while we are on the cash situation
There is a reason leaders would like this nation
To do away with cash and use a card
It reveals how much you earn, what you spend money on
Where you go, what you do, your personal prolegomenon
A perfect way of tracking you, and it's not that hard

You used to be able to talk to a real person in a bank
Who made you welcome, helped see to your needs
Gave you advice, banked your business proceeds
If they keep culling services, I harbour the fear
The local bank and its services will disappear

In days gone by the tradesman came
He did his job and it was our job to pay him
These days it is more complex than that
A sub-contractor who adds credit card tax
Not to mention GST
When problems arise denies liability
Not his responsibility

Oh, how I yearn for the old days to return
When we phoned a business to voice concern
A real person picked up the phone
Reassured us that we were not alone
That the company would walk us through the maze
Listen carefully, problem solve, appraise

Today the Bot puts us on interminable hold
Has us punching in numbers and doing as told
If we're lucky after some lapse of time
A real live operator comes onto the line
Trouble is, can't understand what they say
Because they live in a country far, far away

This technical world is all a mystery to me
And others, who came before the Internet and even TV
The phone rules the roost that can't be denied
People feel bereft without it by their side
It's part of their psyche, their identity
Do you find it scary, or is it just me?

Telecommunication, a journey

Our first telephone was black and attached to the wall
It shrilled loudly to announce every call
You took the ear-piece from the lever
And put it to your ear so you could hear
Then spoke into the receiver
The public phone box was red and serviced most of us
Usually located at the Post Office an institution of great trust
You dialled the number, put in your coin, stated your case succinctly
If your money ran out there was no doubt you would be cut off really quickly

The Melbourne Olympics in 1956 improved telecommunication
Connected Melbourne to London, a miracle of telegraph conjugation
The telephone table in the hall had a phone that matched the décor
A nook for the book that held numbers, addresses and more
It came in four colours - red, beige, black and green - really neat
It sat proudly on a table with its special side seat

However, there was no way of keeping a track
If you missed a telephone call, they had to call you back
The answering machine was a later solution to that
"Hi this is Elsie, please leave a message and I will return the call"
A brief message proudly announced to one and all
This answering device ensured friends never had to phone twice
It decluttered the phone table and made it look nice
Then came a phone with a long, long cord
You could wander around with it, like a knight with a shiny sword
The wireless phone had two or three handsets
Buttons to push and multiple outlets
Then came the car phone as large as a brick
Tradies could sit in their cars and talk on it

The first mobile phone was delicate and brittle
Could only take calls and do texts but it improved little by little
Until a camera was attached
A calculator, a clock, phone and numbers were matched
Then came the phone with a video, email, notebook, calendar
Diary, GPS, bank, word processor
Play station, torch, weather report, calculator
Clock, internet, encyclopedia, access to the world's media
Once the cell phone was invented there was no need for a socket
The smartphone is a mini-computer right there in our pocket
There is no doubt about it we can't live without it
Telecommunications have taken us far, so now this little thing
Does just about everything and more
Minus that first shrill ring

Pending storm

Cold bleak day
Families stay
Inside
Hide
Away from the grey

Still waters mirror silent shadows
No whish of wind stirs the steely sea
Breathe it in, this is how it's meant to be
This calm before the storm
Breaking day delivers dreary dawn
Bleak town by the beach this morn
Birds shelter in their hillside hub
Gossip and chatter up in the scrub
Take refuge from the pending storm
Savour this glorious serenity
This may not always be
Mother nature rules, no certainty

Clouds and sea mist collide and melt
Into each other, one giant blurry pelt
Wind and rain pound, obscure up from down
Yesterday's bright sunshine turned around
King tide
Laps harbour-side
Townsfolk pray rain will subside
Avert overflow and so prevent
Another one-hundred-year flood event

ON LOVE

Ideal man

There is so much to consider when searching for a mate
Because doing life together is a taxing journey to take
This is a most important decision and determines destiny
A wrong choice is disastrous; a good one, a joyful melody
These elements consider in the search for a male prototype
It a race that's made for stayers, not for the sprinting type
If a partnership is to endure and survive for the long haul
You will need to learn to give and take, forgive and so much more
The one thing that's essential is compatibility
For without that a life of peace is an impossibility
Most women love a man who can make her laugh
Making the journey fun for two along life's rocky path
A light touch and a lively imagination can overcome so much
A generous soul, a daring spirit, a kind and gentle touch
A man who loves the family and who plays with his offspring
Who is not afraid to be himself, who lets his spirit sing
He must be loyal and faithful and easy to trust
Nurturing what you have together so it doesn't grow stale and rust
A woman loves a man who does his fair share of the chores
Takes responsibility for himself, both outside and indoors
A good man will nurture and share love every single day
He loves you the way you are and hopes you stay that way

The ark of love

Our ship was portside, what could we do?
Let it sail without us, or become part of the crew?
If we let this one go, maybe another would come along
Or it could well be that what was gone was gone
Either way, the risk was ours to take
So we joined hands, jumped aboard and became shipmates
To sail through life together, leaving all in our wake
Left our old lives behind
Our spirits combined
We were two of a kind
The yin and the yang
A new family began

Old love

Love is wonderful when it's brand spanking new
Oblivious to the rest of the world, there is just the two of you
Busy discovering the intimate secrets of each other's soul
Two mortal people united, becoming one whole

New love is an ache in the heart
Whenever two lovers are apart
The joy of seeing each other at the end of the day
Of learning, growing together, and sharing the way
The excitement for what the road up ahead might hold
The joyful anticipation of how life may unfold
It's the thinking about the future and the making of plans
Joys and sorrows shared, the calling of wedding banns
As in ecstatic harmony two bodies in unison join
Creating your very own family, delicious fruits of the loin

Somewhere along the way young love grows old
Quietness descends upon the once busy household
Your seeds have been sown, the children are grown
Just you and your partner at home on your own
No more striving, grateful for each day
The frantic business of youth somehow cast away
Now it's 'me time', a moment for taking stock
History is leaving its imprint, like sand upon the rock

Having shared each other's ups and downs
Sideways twists and round and rounds
You instinctively know what the other will do
Welded closely together, connective tissue
The present us is the sum of our shared past
The knowledge that we are old, that this won't always last

We have done so much together that we have morphed into one
Navigating life's dips and turns until it seems, we have become
Elsie'nGraeme, Nan'nPop, Dad'nMum
For now, we have each other and feel truly blessed
Old love is gentle, it's love at its best

Two ducks

Two ducks mate for life
Then comes strife
Now only one lonely duck
It sucks
How long should she wait
She yearns
For her mate
Will he return?
Or has she been spurned?
Has he been harmed?
Has he gone away?
She will stay calm
And return each day
In the hope that he will come back
To their pool-side cul de sac

The Yarram Football Club Ball

The whole town looked forward to the footy club ball
An event held annually in the Regent Theatre Hall
The team members gathered, resplendent in suits
Dressed to the nines down to snazzy cowboy boots

The town girls knew this was their moment to impress
They tizzed up their hair, applied lipstick, and in best evening dress
Made their way to the theatre, eagerly anticipating the big event
Balloons, red and white, Darnett's Big Band, the entertainment

The ladies in the kitchen fussed over sandwiches, pies and cakes
The older men manned the door and organised sweepstakes
This was the team's major fund-raising event
To ensure survival next year and for moneys already spent

She went with her friend, he with his brother
They met and hit it off, enthralled with each other
Cupid's bow struck and when others went home, the young couple danced on and on
Until he leaned in and whispered, 'Would you like to hear some of me poems?'

No other man had asked her this, so she was quietly fascinated
She instinctively knew he was different to other boys she had dated
'This bloke is interesting,' she thought, 'not like all the rest
'I'll give him a chance, see what he's got.' And so she answered, 'Yes'

That was the beginning of things to come
Tightly sealed when he took her home to meet his mum
Who said, 'I like her, she suits you, she has got lots of class
'If you're wise, son, you'll marry that little blue-eyed lass'

An engagement ring, a wedding day, later a bun in the oven
The beginning of an eventful life full of laughter and loving
And three more kids to follow and grandkids galore
Life gave that lucky pair all they could ever want, and lots more

ON MELBOURNE

Melbourne in spring time

Along bush paths wattle heralds that winter's end is drawing near
Their final blaze of golden glory announces that spring is all but here
Wandering wisteria and magnificent magnolia don glorious gowns
Determined to be first in show, here today but tomorrow gone

Pink and white plum blossoms ride the wind and their magic sprinkle
Gardens come alive with colour, insect friends intermingle
Birds and grey nomads return from their northern winter hideaways
Having avoided dank winter months, they head home for warmer days

Football finals played and won, the Grand Final the annual climax
People venture out of home to sit in the sun and relax
Keen gardeners head to Bunnings to replenish plants and soil
Water-craft are hauled from storage, engines cleaned and oiled
Cobwebs removed, windows cleaned, garden furniture revived
Scrub the BBQ, check the pool toys, have they managed to survive?

Melbourne Spring is the season of hope and joyful anticipation
Of windy squalls, warm sunny spells, intermittent precipitation
Spring holds secrets tightly within her budding centrefold
Of the joyful promise of how the coming summer will unfold

Melbourne in winter

As cold, drab, grey, winter draws
Close the curtains, shut the blinds. Keep nice and warm indoors
Heaters, doonas, overcoats and jumpers go on
Slow cooked comfort food, jam and cream and scone
Last leaves of autumn colour flutter all around
Rain, sleet and frost make them slippery slides upon the ground
Rug up, take a brisk walk by the bay
Watch seagulls catch the upward drifts and fly away
Don your team's footy stripes, off to see the game
Huddle near the boundary line, trusting it won't rain
Visit the local library, stock up on reading matter
A glass of claret by the fire, settle in for a good long natter
The thing about winter in Melbourne that I love so much
Is just when you've had enough of the chill and such
And the cold starts to become a drudge
Making you think things are pretty tough
The sun sneaks a furtive peep from behind a cloud
Bestows a sunny couple of hours just to make us glad
It breaks the cycle of wind and rain
Gives us hope, keeps us sane
Until it visits us again

Melbourne in autumn

Days draw in as winter's cloak descends
Morning dawns, still dark, daylight saving ends
Sun yawns and rises over silent, still bay
Sea mist hangs low at the start of day
Melbourne in autumn is optimal time
Sublime

Sweet salvias sway underneath the tired trees
Final days for honey, buzz the busy working bees
The trees, having shaded us through summer sizzle
Relax, colour, release their grip on the mother tree and frizzle
At peace now that their job is done
Basking in faint autumn sun
Melbourne in the autumn time
Sublime

Gold, russet, red and brown, leaves softly spent on the ground
Birds raking for worms, the rustling sound
As they scratch and last songs of summer sing
Nights draw in, easing summer's searing sting
Southern autumn transcends northern spring
Melbourne in the autumn time
Sublime

Balmy summer moves north, retreats
Winter storms south, they meet and greet
The chill gets brisker every day
Summer now so far away.
Sleep comes more easily
Snuggle under the doona so peacefully
Melbourne in autumn is the optimal time
Sublime

Melbourne on a summer's day

What's not to love about a Melbourne summer's day?
With winter long departed, spring has paved the way
Now the summer sun energises us
Nature's brilliant pallet tantalizes us
Caressing us, chasing aches and pains away

Summer brings a sense of warmth and wellbeing
That in bleak winter we could not have foreseen
Chatty birds and buzzy bees
Take shelter in the shrubs and trees
Uniting in a' Capella chorus
Singing of long days before us

Tender eyes squint at the skies
As the horizon heats and waters vaporise
Sun's silent sizzle burns fair skin
Splish, splash, splosh, ready to dive in
To cooling waters, pool, surf, dam and river
Aquatic sports and games defeat hot weather

By day glaring light of Australian summer shines
Come evening soft breezes waft, gentle valentines
Blowing cool and soft at the end of day
Making windchimes sing, taking the heat away

Melbourne, the world's most liveable city

Melbourne is much more than trams, the city centre, laneways and endless bustle
Arcades, Southbank, shops, cafes and restaurants, a hub of humming hustle
Melbourne has an inner life, a gracious tranquillity
Elegant buildings, parks and gardens, avenues lined with trees

The Yarra and Maribyrnong snake their way to where Melbournians thrive
Family homes with yards and nature strips, all within a one-hour drive
No matter what your preference, suburban or inner city
The choice is yours, what do you want? Serene or nitty gritty
The inner suburbs are full of life with students and professionals
Bars, cafes, restaurants, theatres, music and just about everything else
Intertwined with places that are down on their luck and faded
Past history written on the walls, her underbelly crazy and jaded
Inner Bayside's beachy feel celebrates newfound wealth and position
Speak loudly and enunciate, regard interlopers with suspicion

The Heidelberg School of artists erected their easels 'round Mentone
Bayside beauty down Edithvale way makes it a desirable place for a home
Long Beach stretches from Mordialloc to Bonbeach and then some more
To suburban Frankston City, gateway to playgrounds on the Peninsula
On the other side of the West Gate Bridge is the pretty port of Williamstown
Altona, Ascot Vale, Werribee and Point Cook, along to Geelong and all round
Venture north and west for a vibrant vortex of effervescent ethnicity
Food, language, cultures and colour mingle and clash with magnificent multiplicity

The very proper eastern quarter is home to wealth and old school ties
While at the foot of the Dandenong Ranges native fauna and flora are highly prized
Here, children play in the street
And run through garden sprinklers in the heat
On the fringes of suburbia living on large hobby-farm blocks
Are suburbanites who own a horse and prefer to live without locks
We Melbournians are a diverse mob and can't simply be placed in boxes
We share a love of the place we live, its moods and paradoxes
Let's not mention the weather and our four seasons in one day
Five million people call Melbourne home. Our dear city by the Bay.

Beautiful Beaumaris by the sea

We came to Melbourne as raw country kids
Outsiders not attached to locale
We made the decision as to where we would live
By buying a house at an auction sale
How lucky were we
That it happened to be
Beautiful Beaumaris by the sea
We had looked at other places and thought of living there
But we hadn't the budget, there was no money to spare
So we put in an offer on a two bedroomed beach shack
Was accepted, moved in, and never looked back
The Bay laps at one end and the Nepean Highway at the other
Our little enclave is an island, away from noise and clutter
Native trees and tea-tree hug homes and guard all inside
Tennis, golf, water sports and beaches within a bicycle ride
As many shops as you could ever need, the fresh sea breeze
Nothing better than beautiful Beaumaris by the sea

ON REFLECTION

Why?

Why do I have empathy
With live meat trade sheep
While what happens to our refugees
Doesn't bother me?

Why do I have sympathy
For the great white whale
While men imprisoned on Manus
Are treated reprehensibly?

Why do we fail to see
Our differences do not define us?
Refugees are like you and me
Reject white supremacy
Instead share our humanity

We are all one, you and me
Why do we feel no shame
For policy made in our name
That disregards empathy
Shows no sympathy
For asylum seeker pain?

Bounce-back-ability

The essence of resilience
Is to view each new experience
With joyful positivity
And unbending flexibility
In the light of good or bad
Happy, dire or sad
Apply dogged capability
With mental agility
Solve the conundrum
Tackle the problem
Head on
Be strong
Respond
With bounce-back-ability

Lucky us

Australia's the land of sunshine, dust storms, wind and torrential rain
Bushfires, floods, droughts, magnificent beaches and rugged terrain
Our sharks attack swimmers, we have a multitude of poisonous snakes and spiders
It sounds pretty scary if you stop to think, but not for us lucky insiders
We know that these things are not the sum of it all
It's the best country on earth. There, I've made a big call
How grateful I am to my people before
Who left their own countries and came to our shore
And settled and prospered and made Oz their own
A great place to live, a wonderful home

I'm glad that I have travelled the world and discovered
Australia stands head and shoulders above all the others
We have sunshine, fresh air and space, all of which is free
Education is available to all, so we can be who we want to be
Perhaps not all is perfect but if you take time to pause and reflect
And examine almost every aspect
When all is put to any test
We Aussies are blessed
The luckiest!

I am Aussie

What does it mean to be an Aussie
Is it fresh air and sunshine that sets us free?
What makes us Aussies different from the rest
Is it that we know deep down that we are truly blessed?

Our indigenous proudly possess the oldest continuous culture on earth
They suffered when white fellow invaded, greatly demeaning their worth
Their pride diminished, but that is all finished, their culture is being proclaimed
Their stories are told, their flag is flown, at long last their rights are reclaimed
Our flora and fauna are unique to us and to others may seem absurd
They can't conceive of a duck with fur or the frantic laughter of a bird
Our continent spreads across the zones from tropics to icy snow
We drive four-wheel-drives and SUVs if we have places we wish to go
The Black Stump is way out bush between the Red Centre and Kakadu
While Woop Woop is west of the Birdsville Track, way beyond Uluru
The Ghan takes three days to snake its way up north
The Indian Pacific takes eight days to travel back and forth

Our country is huge, the people diverse, its amazing vistas so varied
But there are some things that only we Aussies in our genetics carry
As kids we play local rules cricket in our back yards by choice
While mum hangs the washing out to dry on the iconic Hills Hoist
"No hat, no play" is the golden rule of the primary school playtime
Cicadas sing loudly in the heat around about Christmastime
The Royal Flying Doctor tends to patients in the far Outback
Grey Nomads wander in mobile homes over the Gibb River track

We spread salty Vegemite on our sandwiches and toast
Enjoy a snag on the weekend barbie and in winter, a Sunday roast
We chose to fly Qantas if we have to go anywhere
And outback folk wear Akubra hats made from rabbit hair
We splash ourselves with sunscreen and apply zinc onto our noses
Spray the Mortein and Aerogard all around to fend off mozzies
We have our own way of speaking, an Aussie turn of phrase
Strangers find it hard to comprehend our English changing ways

We shorten names, we lengthen nouns, and we loudly proclaim, "You beaut!"
When we brush bush flies from our face we perform our national salute
We greet you with, "How ya goin' mate?' or perhaps a simple "G'day!"
We use rhyming slang whenever we can and if we don't want to do it, "No way!"
We dig great riches from the ground and ship them to third world countries
Ignoring sustainable energy options and making us dirty coal junkies
We experience droughts and flooding rains and raging bushfires
Yet our Government wears the ignorant cloak of climate change deniers

Simple things

If I could organise the world, there's a few things I would change
Some things I would leave right alone, others I would rearrange
I've had my three score years plus ten and am living past my time
It gives me space to pause, reflect, and form my personal paradigm
My greatest hate was compatriots who interfered in other people's lives
And everything that goes with war, greed, and leaders who told lies
These things I would prohibit and banish from this planet
But there are lots of things that I would keep, if I could only do it
I loved warm summer evenings sitting out with family and friends
Simple things, picnics and swims, camping on weekends
I loved a cold winter's day and a walk upon the beach
The whiff of recently cut hay, the smell of a fresh ripe peach
The soft pink haze that touches the trees at sunset before twilight
The kindness of a stranger, a good soul who tries to make things right
The filtered light that shines in on you early in the morning
The birds busy with their lives loudly announcing the dawning
My bed before the lights are dimmed, so soft and cosy and warm
The feeling that I'm safe and sound and away from all real harm
A lie-in on a Saturday at the end of a busy week
Hours spent playing with children, a game of hide and seek
The family at home with you, safe behind closed doors
A hearty laugh with friends who tolerate your flaws
Working in the garden the whole year round
Planting seeds, trimming back, digging in the ground
A glass of wine, good company, a trip into the country
Becoming the best that you can be, all these things are dear to me
But the things that stand out boldly and alone
Are the simple things that were there for me in my own sweet home

AND FINALLY

Poetry of sorts has always been a thing in our family. The night we first met, at the footy club ball, the young man who was to become my beloved sparked my interest with the phrase, 'Would you like to hear some of me poems?'
I had never heard that as a conversation starter before!
He continued to woo me with the odd 'masterpiece' here and there and once we established our own family there followed birthday poems, Christmas poems, Tooth Fairy poems, holiday poems and poems 'just because'.
I found I also enjoyed writing poetry. I liked the discipline of searching and finding the right word, making a line scan, finding a rhyme, expressing a thought or emotion.
Poems became commonplace and as expected, the butt of many family jokes. And that is where these two anchor poems came into play.
I wrote the first one and surprise, surprise, instead of sending it up, my granddaughter responded. I couldn't have been happier.

All about anchors

Embrace your world with joy, love, humour and curiosity
Make and own your decisions, create a personal philosophy
We are all in our own boats to sail as we will
Keep the anchor at the ready and hands firmly on the tiller
Surf life's storms, gales and squalls, remember this reality
Your safe harbour is your home
and
Your anchor is your family

In a harbour snug where waters play
An anchor rests in dawn's soft grey
Tethered firm to the ocean's foam
It echoes tales of a longed for home
Beside the hearth where embers glow
A refuge found, a haven stow
A dog named Ruby loyal and true
Guardian of memories I did strew
Through storms that rage and winds that howl
Ruby's bark a comforting yowl
A tether to hearts that sometimes roam
An anchor's song, a dog and home

- Verity Wilson

Books by Elsie Johnstone

Our Little Town, Growing Up in Lakes Entrance, 2009
Lover Husband Father Monster - Her Story, 2010
Ma's Garden, 2012
Around The Kitchen Table, 2012
Rainbow Over Narre Warren, 2014
Lover Husband Father Monster - The Aftermath, 2015
Come On Victoria, I'm Done – poems about COVID, 2021

The 'Girl' Trilogy

Lakes Entrance girl - Collected Poems, 2020
Catholic girl - Collected Poems, 2020
Old girl - Collected Poems, 2024

www.ingramcontent.com/pod-product-compliance
Lightning Source LLC
Chambersburg PA
CBHW072020290426
44109CB00018B/2295